Boots the of Notti

on old pictur... ......

Brian Marchant

Miss *PUSS* in

Why not Follow her Example this Christmas Time?

1. Early 1900's Christmas advertising postcard for Boots Cash Chemists. Publisher unknown.

Introduction

This book includes a selection of postcards from a collection depicting the development of Boots The Chemists over the 20th century. Boots is one of the UK's leading retailers and a household name. Furthermore, The Boots Company PLC, in addition to retailing, includes product development and manufacturing, international marketing and property management businesses.

It was, though, the tiny shop in Goose Gate, Nottingham, opened by John and Mary Boot and selling herbal remedies, which was to become the foundations of one of the largest retailers in the UK. In a book on Nottingham by Francis White & Co 1853, John Boot is listed as a Medical Botanist of 6, Goose Gate, Nottingham.

Jesse Boot, born on 2 June, 1850 was the first child of John and Mary Boot and following the early death of his father in 1860, he left school at the age of 13 to help his mother run the shop. As the young Jesse gained experience in the shop, he began to take an increasing share in its management. In 1871, at the age of 21, Jesse was given a partnership in the business which was to trade under the name of Mary & Jesse Boot, herbalists. In 1877 Jesse took control of the business from his mother and this became the basis for the origins of The Boots Company.

Jesse's early philosophy to cut prices to the minimum was a reflection of his background of working and living in Hockley, one of the poorest areas in Nottingham. His reputation for dealing in cash was later used in the company title *Boots Cash Chemists,* which featured prominently on many stores up to the early 1900's: some early examples of these are illustrated in this book.

A House of Lords judgement in 1879 ruled that anyone dispensing medicines had to be a qualified chemist, and this led Boots to employ its first pharmacist in 1883. Jesse's new store in Goose Gate, Nottingham opened in 1884 and marked the beginning of his expansion plans. However, Jesse Boot's health continued to deteriorate as a result of continued overwork, and following a complete breakdown in 1885 he was forced to take an extended holiday in Jersey. There Jesse met Florence Rowe, the daughter of a bookseller and stationer, and they were married in 1886. His wife soon developed a keen interest in the business and was directly responsible for the development of the Boots Stationery and Fancy goods department.

In 1888 Jesse Boot formed the Boots Pure Drug Company Ltd to manufacture products for the stores. His initial intentions were to control the price and quality of every product sold in a Boots store. In 1892, Jesse opened a new shop at a prime town centre site on the corner of Pelham Street and High Street, Nottingham. This first "department" store, selling stationery, books, fancy goods, toiletries, and dispensing medicines became a model for future department stores throughout the country.

During the early 1890's, Florence Boot, with her interest in literature and the arts, founded the Boots Book Lovers Library and the development of cafés in Boots larger stores. These innovations helped improve the image of the stores and attracted the "middle classes". Florence was probably responsible for the company's early issue of postcards of Nottingham, sold from the Pelham Street store. As postcards became popular at the end of the 19th century, the larger Boots stores began to issue topographical cards of the surrounding area. These were published under the "Pelham" series imprint, initially by Boots Cash Chemists (later Boots The Chemists or Boots Pure Drug Co Ltd). Other cards published by Boots included a "real photographic" series from about 1907 and others under specific trademarks registered by the company. Subjects included military and patriotic, along with artist-drawn views. One Sheffield-born artist,Walter Hayward Young ("Jotter"), designed at least 84 scenes which were published as postcards by Boots. All the postcards, whether photographs of Boots stores, local views, birthday cards etc, helped to advertise the Boots name across the country. The earliest Boots postcard so far noted is a sepia view of Trent Bridge, Nottingham, postmarked in 1899.

Jesse soon wished to find premises to expand the wholesale and manufacturing functions. He basically wanted to be self-sufficient and be the *"largest, best and cheapest"* chemists in the whole country. He eventually moved into

Island Street, which ran along the centre of a virtual island formed by the Nottingham canal basin, and soon developed this area for manufacturing and warehousing. Later he extended by purchasing premises in Station Street. In 1898 Boots leased space in a building on Station Street, previously Hine & Mundella's steam-powered hosiery factory, for office purposes, and in 1912 he bought the whole factory. Jesse Boot's own office was on the first floor over the main entrance.

By 1902 the company had over 270 shops and sales had reached one million pounds. This led Jesse to claim the *"Largest Cash Chemists in the World"*, a slogan which appeared in bold letters over some of his shops.

In the period up to the First World War, Boots embarked upon a period of rapid development of manufacturing and warehouse activities in Nottingham to keep pace with the expansion of the stores, and the philosophy of Jesse Boot that he could manufacture his own proprietary lines cheaply, advertise them widely and still produce a small profit margin. During the period 1914-1918 there was a major wartime investment in manufacturing capacity. Boots established research and development capability, producing synthetic chemicals as part of the war effort.

As Jesse became tired from years of exhaustive work, strain of the war and the worsening of his arthritis, which he had suffered with since about 1910, he began to think about selling the company.

In 1920 he sold Boots to Louis Liggett, the head of the United Drug Company, one of the largest firms in the USA, for £2.25 million, with a year's dividend to be paid to Jesse. There then followed a period of reorganisation, and with Jesse's son John Boot's help, Louis Liggett introduced a more modern system of management into Boots and a period of rapid development took place over the next ten years, with John Boot largely responsible.

Jesse Boot, as titular chairman, had virtually no responsibilities within the new company, and devoted a great deal of time during this period to the provision of a site and a large proportion of the cost of a new university in Nottingham, which was opened by King George V and Queen Mary in 1928. Soon after Jesse Boot became "Lord Trent of Nottingham".

John Boot, continued the visionary project started by Jesse in the early 1920's to build a new manufacturing plant in the early 1920's, leading to the development of a major industrial complex at Beeston with the construction of a Soap Works and first class facilities for the production of "Wet" & "Dry" goods. Land was also bought nearby for future development of the company.

In 1931 Jesse Boot died, and two years later John Boot, with support from influential bankers, was able to buy back the company from Louis Liggett of the United Drug Company, USA. In the same year the magnificent "Wets" Factory (D10) Beeston, designed by Sir Owen Williams, was opened and also Boots opened its 1000th store. John Boot continued to expand the company, and by the time of his death in 1956 Boots The Chemists was one of the leading companies in the UK.

Boots continued to expand by acquisition, and in 1968 bought the Timothy Whites and Taylors Chemist chain of over 600 stores. Further major retailing expansion followed with the acquisition of the Ward White Companies in 1989. In 1995 Boots sold its Pharmaceutical business to BASF, Germany.

Today Boots is a company with interests worldwide and sales of over five billion pounds. It is a leading retailer, has one of the largest property portfolios in the UK and is a leader in the development, manufacture and marketing of healthcare and consumer products. From a tiny shop in Hockley to the opening of its first store in Japan, surely Jesse Boot's vision has been realised.

Brian Marchant
November 1999

Front cover: The 'Wets' factory (DIO), Beeston, shortly after its official opening in 1933. Designed by Sir Owen Williams, this 'Industrial Palace' has been described as a milestone in modern architecture. It remains Boots' premier manufacturing facility today.

PELHAM STREET, NOTTINGHAM

2. Pelham Street, Nottingham, with Boots' Pelham Street store on the right. Originally opened in 1884, this became a 'model' for future Boots department stores throughout the country, and remained a Boots shop until 1972. Jigsaw the retailers now trade from these premises.

St. Peter Street, Derby

Valentines Series

Here is another one of Derby for You.

3. St. Peter Street, Derby c. 1900, showing an early Boots shop on the left, on the corner of St. Peter's churchyard. This site was purchased by Jesse Boot in 1894, and a new Boots store was built near East Street in 1912. The famous Midland Drapery Magnet sign is clearly visible on the right. This postcard was published by Valentine of Dundee, one of Britain's earliest and most major postcard publishers, and was posted to Hampstead in August 1903.

4. Looking northwards up Mansfield Road, Nottingham c. 1904, with a Boots shop at 1, Mansfield Road (at the corner of Shakespeare Street) near the present YMCA. This shop was opened at the YMCA buildings in 1897, and extended the following year to the corner of Shakespeare Street. It is here advertising Bovril and 'Aerated Water' (Boots were manufacturers of mineral water in the early 1900's). The shop was closed in the mid-1970s, and the site is now occupied by the Sony Centre.

5. Early Nottingham Boots Cash Chemists shop on Carrington Street, adjacent to the 'Portland Hotel.' It is seen here on a c. 1907 postcard published by Bamforth of Holmfirth, better known as publishers of saucy comic cards. The store in this area was opened at 1 Arkwright Street in 1896, but in 1901 was closed for the redevelopment of the Midland Railway Station and relocated to Carrington Street. By 1909, its address was Carrington Street Bridge. It closed in 1941 because of the war. This store's number, 17, was transferred to the shop opened on the newly-built Clifton Estate in 1954. It is now located at 222/4 Southchurch Drive, Clifton.

Market Place, Loughborough.

High Street, Banbury.

6. Market Street, Loughborough on a card published in Boots' "Pelham" Series and posted at Loughborough in January 1905. The Boots store on the right is an example of one containing a library, a concept founded by Florence Boot. It was opened at 1 Biggin Street in 1895, but the address was changed to 10 Market Place in 1898. Current address is 11/13 Market Place *(see illus. 43 for a 1950's view of the shop).*

7. High Street, Banbury, showing in the centre an early Boots store emblazoned with *Boots Cash Chemists* across the front of the building and from the rooftops. 'Book Lovers Library' also appears in large letters. The site is now occupied by a Dorothy Perkins shop. "Pelham" series card, published in August 1906.

8. A Boots-published postcard of Newborough, Scarborough, showing a Boots store on the right advertising *Cash Chemists, Perfumers and Book Lovers Library.*

9. A view of High Steet, Guildford, showing a Boots store on the right with *Boots Cash Chemists, Book Lovers Library* displayed across the building. The card, published in the Boots "Pelham" series, was posted in Farnham in December 1906.

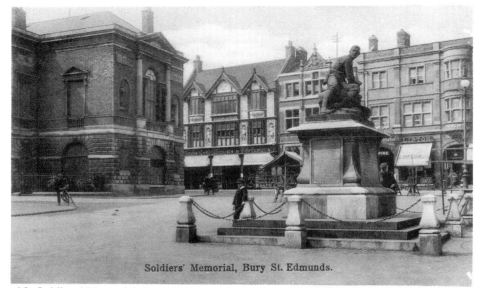

Soldiers' Memorial, Bury St. Edmunds.

10. Soldiers' Memorial, Bury St Edmunds. In the early 1900's, Boots Cash Chemists and Perfumers was located in the Tudor style building shown just to the left of the memorial in Cornhill. W.H. Smith now occupy the building, while a modern Boots store is located further down Cornhill. Card in Boots' own "Pelham" series.

Tavern Street, Ipswich.

11. Boots Cash Chemists and Stationers at 22 Tavern Street, Ipswich, around 1905, the year after the shop opened. It has a typical ornate lamp used by Boots shops of the period. This shop was extended to the corner of Tavern Street and St Lawrence Street in 1929, further extended in 1952, and closed in 1986.

12. View of Fargate, Sheffield, showing an early Boots store on the left. The first Boots branch outside Nottingham was opened in Sheffield in 1884. Card postally used in September 1909.

13. Postcard of High Street, Newmarket, showing a Boots Cash Chemists store on the left with the words *Chemists and Perfumers* displayed above the shop windows. The card was published in Boots' "Real Photograph" series and posted at Thetford in September, 1907. The sender was not complimentary: *"This is a place. Only one P.H.* (public house). *Have come 4 miles without a drink."*

High Street, Market Harborough.

14. High Street, Market Harborough showing a Boots shop on the left. *Cash Chemists and Perfumers* is displayed over the shop front. Another Boots-published card.

The Angel Hotel, Grantham

15. This postcard shows a Boots Cash Chemists and Stationers adjacent to The Angel Hotel, Grantham. Published in the "Pelham" series and postmarked from Grantham in August 1907, it was sent to Boston with the message *"it was lovely at Wyville yesterday, we drove there and back in a trap."*

16. Briggate, Leeds showing an early Boots store just to the right of the centre of the card. Boots originally acquired a site in Briggate in 1901 and began the expansion into rivals "Taylors" territory. Published by Valentine and posted at Leeds in August 1909.

17. Scene from High Street, Putney showing typical transport at that time. On the left can be seen scaffolding with the *'Built for Boots'* display. Published by Hutchinson and Co, Wimbledon, and posted in Putney in June 1909.

18. View of High Street, Chesterfield with the famous 'leaning spire' in the centre. Card published by Boots in the "Pelham" series and posted in Saffron Walden in July, 1908. On the right is a Boots Cash Chemist and Stationers advertising *Picture Framers, Toilet Requisites, Perfumers and 'The Largest Retail Chemists in the World'*.

19. A postcard, published by Valentine, of Hightown, Hereford in the early 1900's. The Boots store on the right displays in large letters *"Boots The Largest Retail Chemists in the World"*. It opened at 28 High Town in 1897, and transferred to its current address, 12/13 High Street and 42/43 Bewell Street, about 1970.

20. Early 1900's postcard of the Corn Exchange, Luton. On the right is a small Boots store with *Chemists and Stationers* printed on one side and on the front *"Boots, Largest, Best, Cheapest, Chemists in the World"*.

21. An early 1900's card from the "Caledonia" series (published by J.A. McCulloch & Co.), posted in Glasgow. The view is Sauchiehall Street, Glasgow, showing in the centre of the card a building displaying Boots Chemists - *"Largest Cash Chemists in the World"*.

22. Oldham Street, Manchester, with a Boots Cash Chemists on the left. The store is advertising as *Stationers, Picture Framers and Builders* with the words *"Circulating Library"* displayed on the window. Boots opened its first shop in Manchester in Oldham Street in 1897. Another Boots "Pelham" series card c. 1910.

23. View of the Market Place, Gainsborough, on market day, with a Boots Cash Chemists store clearly visible on the left. Card published by Valentine.

24. View of Salisbury Street, Blandford, in Dorset. A good example of an early Boots Cash Chemists is shown on the left with the store advertising Drugs and Gifts. The postcard was published by Boots themselves.

25. "Pelham" series postcard of George Street, Croydon, showing a Boots Cash Chemists on the right. The card was posted on 11th August 1914. *"Dear Nellie, there has been great excitement over choosing and writing these postcards. Only Basil has gone away at present."* This was presumably a reference to the departure of soldiers at the start of the First World War.

26. Market Place, Macclesfield, showing in the centre a Boots Cash Chemists corner location. *"Circulating Library"* is displayed on the window. Published in the "Dearden" series and postally used in June 1915.

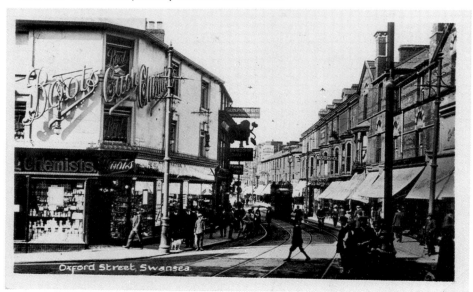

27. A view of Oxford Street, Swansea, showing on the left a Boots store with Boots Cash Chemists prominently displayed across the building. Above the shop windows *'Chemists and Stationers'* is advertised. "Pelham" series postcard, posted in October 1917.

28. Busy scene in Leeming Street, Mansfield. A Boots The Chemists shop is shown on the left. Postcard published by C & A.G. Lewis and postmarked 8th November 1925.

29. Real photographic card of Argyle Street, Glasgow in the early 1900's showing a Boots Pure Drugs store on the right.

30. An unusual example of an early Boots Cash Chemists
as yet unidentified, has prominent adverts for Erasmus Wi

...rtising drugs and gifts. This well stocked store, location
...scing Salt and Cascara Capsules.

LEIGH ROAD. EASTLEIGH. HANTS.

31. View of Leigh Road, Eastleigh, Hampshire, with a Boots Cash Chemists on the right. The sign *Perfumery and Toilet Requisites* is displayed above the shop. Published by A. Churchill, 48, Southampton Road, Eastleigh and posted in July 1919.

OLD MARKET. HALIFAX.

32. View of the Old Market, Halifax showing a Boots Cash Chemists store advertising *pure drugs and chemicals, gifts and prescriptions dispensed*. Card published by Lilywhite Ltd and posted in January 1928.

33. Postcard posted in Coventry on 14th August 1925, showing a view of Bristol Bridge and High Street. A prominent advert for Boots is displayed on the right with the words *'For value, quality and your utmost satisfaction always shop at Boots'*. The display board also states *'Over 780 branches throughout Great Britain'*.

AN AERIAL VIEW OF THE PHARMACEUTICAL FACTORIES OF BOOTS PURE DRUG CO. LTD. AT BEESTON, NOTTINGHAM.

34. This postcard shows an aerial view of the pharmaceutical factories of Boots Pure Drug Company Ltd at Beeston, Nottingham. These factories were the largest group of their kind in Europe. Designed by Sir Owen William, Sir Henry Tanner and Boots own architects' department.

35. A rare example of a card showing a Boots store in Blackpool on fire in October, 1937. Publisher unknown.

36. Market Square, Retford, Nottinghamshire. A Boots shop is shown to the right of the War Memorial with the sign above the shop *'Dispensing Chemists'* and *'Toilet Specialists'*. Published in the 1950's by Arjay Productions.

37. Bridge Street, Worksop. Bearing in mind the acquisition of Halford's, as part of the Ward White Companies in 1989, note the proximity of the Boots store and an early Halford's store on the left of the street. Bridge Street is now pedestrianised, and modern Boots and Halford stores have been built on the original sites. Card published by Valentine.

38. Northgate, Wakefield, showing on the left a good example of the *Boots The Chemists* logo style of that time. *Prescriptions dispensed and toilet requisites* are advertised over the shop. Real photographic card published by Lilywhite Ltd.

39. An example of a "Pelham" postcard featuring a Boots store on the corner of Biggin Street, Dover. Besides the prominent advert for *"Films"* one shop window is devoted entirely to Fancy and Silver Goods.

40. High Street, Cheadle, showing an older style Boots Chemists shop in the centre. A banner with the slogan *'Boots For Films'* is displayed from the building. The card was published by Lilywhite Ltd., Sowerby Bridge and postmarked 19th October 1939.

41. A view of The Square, Beeston, Nottingham with the Boots store shown on the right displaying the banner *'Boots for developing & printing'*. Boots was a leader in this field at the time and this has continued to the present day. The card was published by Valentine & Sons Ltd.

42. Reform Street, Dundee showing a typical corner street location on the left for a Boots store. *Toilet Goods and Dispensing Chemists* is displayed above the shop. This postcard was published by Valentine of Dundee and posted in September 1937.

43. Typical early 1950's view of Loughborough with a Boots Dispensing Chemists on the left. In the foreground is a *Leicester Evening Mail* van. Card published by Frith of Reigate.

44. View of Gold Street, Northampton showing a large Boots The Chemists store on the right advertising *Artists materials* in one shop window. This store opened at 38 Gold Street in 1896, moving to 6 Gold Street and 2 The Drapery in 1904, and to its present address, 9 The Parade, in 1975.

45. Postcard published by a London firm, posted in Canterbury in July 1948. The card shows the Cathedral (through Mercery Lane) and a Boots store located on the corner of Parade.

46. View of High Street, Exeter. A typical example of a mid-1950's Boots Dispensing Chemists is shown on the left. Published by E.T.W. Dennis & Sons of London and Scarborough.

HIGH STREET, EAST, WALLSEND.

G.3912.

47. A view of High Street, East, Wallsend, with a large Boots Cash Chemists shown on the corner of Station Road. Displayed in the shop window is the advert *'Prescriptions Carefully Dispensed*'! This was certainly a continuation of the exacting standards originally laid down by Edwin Waring, appointed by Jesse Boot to manage the dispensing side of the business.

NCT 38

CRAINGER STREET, NEWCASTLE-ON-TYNE

A TUCK CARD

48. View of Grainger Street, Newcastle-On-Tyne. On the right is a Boots Dispensing Chemists, advertising *Day and Night Service*. The postcard was published by Raphael Tuck and Sons, Britain's premier postcard firm.

49. Albert Street, Kirkwall. On the left is a small Boots Dispensing Chemists shop, the only Boots in the Orkneys and one of the most northerly stores in the retail chain. A shop is still located in Albert Street today. Published by Valentine & Sons Ltd.

50. High Street, Tunstall. A typical corner site for Boots The Chemists is shown on the right. *Dispensing Chemists and Toilet Specialists* is displayed above the shop windows. Postcard published by Frith of Reigate.

CHURCH STREET, ORMSKIRK.

51. View of Church Street, Ormskirk. A small Boots Chemists shop is shown left of centre with a display board advertising *National Insurance Dispensing*. The passing of the National Health Insurance Act in 1911 extended medical benefits to ordinary working people and increased business for Boots dispensing branches. Card published by Frith.

52. Card published by Valentine of Dundee and posted in November 1960, featuring a view of High Street, Burton-on-Trent. On the left is a Boots *(Dispensing Chemists and Toilet Specialists)* with a café and restaurant. This was another idea originally fostered by Florence Boot to *"attract the fashionable middle classes to shop at Boots."*

53. Card posted in August 1974 showing a view of Pride Hill, Shrewsbury. Prominently featured is a Boots Cash Chemists built in the original Tudor style favoured by Jesse and Florence Boot.

54. A card showing a good example of a large ornate Tudor style Boots store located in the Market Place, Kingston-Upon-Thames. The card is postmarked 22nd August 1968.

55. View of Central Avenue, West Bridgford in the late 1960's showing a Boots The Chemists store on the left. A modern pharmacy store exists on the same site today, adjacent to an HSBC bank. Postcard published by Frith of Reigate.

56. View of High Street and Moat Hall, Keswick, Cumberland. In the centre of the picture is the tiny Moat Hall with its one-handed clock - the hall dates from 1813. A small Timothy White's shop is shown on the left. It became a Boots Dispensing Chemists after Boots acquired the Timothy Whites chain in 1968. Postcard published by H. Webster of Keswick.

57. A typical 1970's style Boots Dispensing Chemists located in Road 2, Fleet. Adjacent to this is a Timothy White's shop, owned by Boots since 1968. The card was published by Roe and Kittredge Ltd of Fleet, Hampshire and posted in July 1977.

No. 72   *Lower Parliament Street*

58. View of Lower Parliament Street, Nottingham. On the right is one of Boots' largest department stores, located in the Victoria Centre, and opened in 1972. This followed the closure of their store in High Street. Card published by Rosamond and Glownia in their "Hockley Coins" series.

59. The pedestrian precinct, Chelmsford, in the mid 1980's. The card shows one of the large modern Boots Dispensing Chemists stores. Photographed by Photo Precision Ltd, St Ives, Huntingdon.

60. Occasion of the visit of King George V and Queen Mary to Nottingham and District, 24 June 1914. An early Boots Stationers and Chemists is shown in the centre but location is unknown.

PRINTED PAPER.

Dispensing Chemists & Toilet Specialists
30, Queen Street,
NEWTON ABBOT.
Telephone : Newton Abbot 230.

We are the LEADING DISTRIBUTORS for all the popular PROPRIETARY MEDICINES and TOILET ARTICLES, including PEARS' TRANSPARENT and PEARS' GOLDEN GLORY Toilet Soaps.

Call and see Pears' wonderful new picture " The Bloom of Youth," on exhibition at this Branch. It is offered **FREE** *to customers in exchange for twelve soap wrappers or cartons. We strongly advise you to secure this charming gift. Our Picture Framing Department will be pleased to frame it for you, complete with glass, at a charge of 3/-.*

MR BUE'E.

1. DEVON SQUARE

NEWTON ABBOT,

61. Postcard issued by Boots The Chemists in Newton Abbot, posted in February, 1931 advertising the picture "The Bloom of Youth" by Russell Flint. This picture was offered free to customers in exchange for twelve soap wrappers or cartons.

The Glory of a Lion is his Mane.

COPYRIGHT.

62. This tribute to our colonies (design by William Armitage) was published in 'Boots Patriotic Series'. The mane is ingeniously made up from the names of the colonies. Card posted in November, 1914.

63. Boots published many postcards by the artist Walter Hayward Young (Jotter). This one of Newport Arch, Lincoln, was posted at Beeston in June 1911.

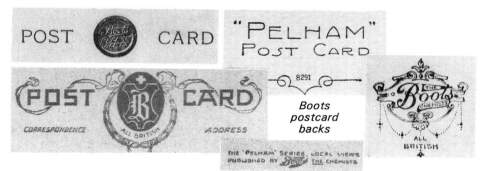

Boots postcard backs

Back cover (top): Real photographic card in the Boots Cash Chemists "Pelham" series showing the stamping room at Boots Christmas Card Department. The card was postally used in January, 1913.

(bottom): Boots General Offices, Station Street, Nottingham. The building was previously Hine and Mundella's hosiery factory, built in 1851 by T.C. Hine. Jesse Boot bought the whole factory in 1912. This c. 1925 view on a postcard published by C & A.G. Lewis features one of Boots' early delivery vehicles in the street.

Acknowledgments: I should like to thank the Dalkeith Publishing Company, Bournemouth, and Derek Peake for permission to use postcards, David Ottewell and Grenville Jennings for the loan of illustrations, and The Boots Company PLC for their helpful comments and provision of additional information.

Sources and further reading: **Jesse Boot of Boots The Chemists** (Stanley Chapman). Hodder & Stoughton 1974.
A Cap for Boots: an autobiography (J.E. Greenwood). Hutchinson 1977.
Jesse Boot of Nottingham (Christopher Weir). 1994.